CLASSICAL LIBERALISM IN AFRICA

CLASSICAL LIBERALISM IN AFRICA

A MANIFESTO

By

GERMINAL G. VAN

Amazon Digital Services, LLC

This book is a work of political analysis. No part of this book may be reproduced, stored in a retrieval system, or transmitted in any form or by any means, including electronic, mechanical, photocopying, microfilming, recording, or otherwise (except for that copying permitted by sections 107 and 108 of the United States Copyright Law and expect by reviewers for the public press), without written permission from the Publisher.

A Manifesto

By the same Author

American Political Culture

Equal Under the Law

Essays On Issues (Volume 1)

Reflection on Identity Politics

The Efficiency of Capitalism

Democratic Socialism On Trial

The Problem of Egalitarianism

Income Inequality and Economics

Market Economy and the State

The Totalitarian State of America

Au Nom De La République Forte

Classical Liberalism in Africa

Table of Contents

About the Author   ix

Acknowledgements   xii

Preface   xiii

Introduction   1

Part I: Political Freedom in Africa   9

Chapter 1: Political Systems   11
and African Governments

Chapter 2: The Rule of Law in   19
African Political Culture

Chapter 3: Political Rights for the People   29

Part II: Economic Freedom in Africa   37

Chapter 4: The Problem of African Socialism   39

Chapter 5: Private Property and Capital   47

Chapter 6: Improvement of the   57
Living Standard in Africa

Part III: Civil Liberties in Africa   67

Chapter 7: Liberty and African
Political Culture   69

Chapter 8: Political Authority
and the African Citizen   79

Conclusion   87

References   91

ABOUT THE AUTHOR

Germinal G. Van is an author, essayist, libertarian scholar, political economist, and philosopher. He is the author of a dozen books including *The Problem of Egalitarianism, Income Inequality and Economics,* and *Au Nom De La République Forte*, which is his first book written in French. He is also a contributing writer to the Mises Institute, the Libertarian Institute, and the Foundation for Economic Education.

Mr. Van holds a bachelor's degree in political science from the Catholic University of America and a master's degree in political management from the George Washington University. *Classical Liberalism in Africa* is his latest book.

Classical Liberalism in Africa

A Manifesto

ACKNOWLEDGEMENTS

The completion of a book takes time and substantial efforts. Moreover, the author; although he is the writer of the manuscript; the work being produced in the book is not solely the result of his unique efforts. It is the contribution of other people who have contributed either directly or indirectly to the production of the manuscript. Therefore, it is important to thank all the individuals who have brought their contribution to the realization of this manuscript.

I'd like to thank three people for their help throughout the process of this book. First, I would like to thank my wife for her unconditional support upon the completion of this book. Secondly, I would like to thank Dr. Keita, Professor of political science at Alabama State University, for his professional contribution upon the elaboration of the substantive ideas of this book. Lastly, I would like to thank my dear friend, Kayiraba Touré for his intellectual insight within the completion of this manuscript. Kayiraba is an alumnus of the Graduate School of Political Management at the George Washington University.

Classical Liberalism in Africa

A Manifesto

PREFACE

The African continent is an interesting place for political, economic and social development to occur. Most African countries are relatively young artificial states. Artificial because the current lines that are being used as borders, are not in reality borders delimited by Africans themselves. These lines we use as borders were determined, designed, and imposed by the Europeans upon us during the Berlin Conference of 1884. As a matter of fact, the ethnic conflicts and tribalism that led to political instability in Africa, were partially created from these artificial borders.

African states are not fundamentally nation-states because the cultural basis of each of these states is not embedded in a common feature that determines the social framework of a civil society. For example, Côte d'Ivoire alone, is not a nation per se but an artificial and manufactured state because a cultural basis was not fundamentally established at the outset of the independence era. Nonetheless, African states are progressively transitioning from artificial states to nations.

After sixty years of independence, most African states have cultivated some cultural characteristics that could determine their national identity. For example, Kenya could be now considered as a nation-state because the Swahili language is the cultural basis that determines the social framework of the Kenyan people despite the many dialects that are spoken across the country. Moreover, Swahili is a language that is not only spoken but it is also written. Consequently, official and administrative documents are written in English and in Swahili. Ethiopia is another example of an African nation-state. Like the Swahili language in Kenya, the Amharic language is the cultural characteristic that also determines the social framework of the Ethiopian people. In Côte d'Ivoire though, French, which is a foreign language, is the administrative and "national" language of the country. Can Cote d'Ivoire thoroughly be considered as a nation-state despite the fact that French is language commonly spoken in the country? The reader will formulate his or her own response upon this question based on his or her own judgment.

Let me remind the reader that Côte d'Ivoire is not the only African country in that situation. But since it is the country that I am originally from, that is why I used it as an example to illustrate my point. Many French-speaking as well as English-speaking African countries are in the same situation. They have neither a common indigenous language nor a common religion as a form of social standardization to determine the cultural basis of their social framework which could make them a nation-state.

What concerns me the most in this book is to understand how economic freedom, the rule of law, political rights and civil liberties, can improve the well-being of African countries. I decided to title this book *Classical Liberalism in Africa: A Manifesto*, because classical liberalism is the political ideology that has helped the economic, political, and social development of many developing countries. A country like Singapore; which is today one of the most advanced countries in Asia, was yet one of the poorest countries in the Asian continent sixty years ago. It has been able to develop itself because it has relied on the elements of classical liberalism to enhance its economic development.

The central argument of this book is based on the assessment that a civil society cannot prosper if it does not operate on promoting the elements of classical liberalism. Economic prosperity cannot take place if there is no political stability and political stability cannot occur if there is no rule of law. Every country on earth that has achieved a self-sufficient level of economic development, has done so by advancing and prioritizing the rule of law as the essential tool to determine prosperity.

Classical Liberalism in Africa

This book was primarily written for an African audience, but it is not solely limited to African people. It is also written for a general and broader audience, for anyone who is interested in political philosophy and economic theory. It seeks to enlighten Africans about the need for classical liberalism as a necessary condition to ascertain economic, political, and social development. Lastly, this book aims to explain to the African layman that classical liberalism is not a political ideology solely designed for Western culture, but an ideology enhanced for human nature regardless of the skin color or the cultural basis of a people.

Germinal G. Van

July 2019

A Manifesto

INTRODUCTION

Classical liberalism is a political ideology that was born in Europe during the late seventeenth century in England, through a book. Like any conventional ideology, classical liberalism was conceptualized and theorized within a book. This book was published by a British physicist in 1689. It is entitled *Second Treatise of Government*, and its author is John Locke.

Second Treatise of Government holds a great significance because it is the fundamental concept of liberalism in the world. However, the conception of liberalism founded by Locke is not a unanimous conception of liberalism. The other conception of liberalism is that of Jean-Jacques Rousseau, theorized in his book *Social Contract* (1762), in which he argued that liberalism can truly be enhanced if members of society surrender their rights to the state and the state in exchange will ensure the protection of these surrendered rights through the enforcement of equality and liberty.

This Rousseauan concept of liberalism is the essence of liberalism used in Continental Europe; in countries such as France, Germany, Italy, Spain and the majority of European countries. The Rousseauan concept of liberalism is interestingly similar to that of Thomas Hobbes to some extent, but unlike Rousseau, Hobbes saw the state as this unavoidable organization that unilaterally governs society regardless of what the general will is or should be.

The concept of liberalism of John Locke is drastically different from that of Jean-Jacques Rousseau. In *Second Treatise of Government,* Locke argued that the individual is entitled to his natural rights and that the role of the state is only to protect these rights and not to deprive the citizen of it. If the citizen were to be deprived of his rights, it shall be through due process and not arbitrarily without any logical justification. The Lockean liberalism is called the "Anglo-Saxon style" of liberalism because it focuses on the sovereignty of the individual. In the Lockean conception of liberty, the sovereignty of the individual can only be ascertained if he is economically and politically free. In other words, Anglo-Saxon liberalism emphasizes on economic freedom, civil liberties, and the rule of law to restrain the power of the state from infringing upon the rights of the individual. Anglo-Saxon liberalism is mainly used in Western countries such as the United Kingdom, the United States, Australia, and Canada.

Classical liberalism has generally been rejected as an ideological model to be embraced in most non-Western societies; and especially in Africa for two reasons. The first reason is based upon the fact that Africans consider classical liberalism as a synthetic imported Western by-product. For the majority of Africans, especially the Pan-Africanists, classical liberalism is the ideology and system of the oppressor, the white European colonizer who wants to maintain his influence upon the African way of life in order to sustain his order. Secondly, the majority of African governments rejected classical liberalism because African political leaders argued that it is an ideology that is simply not conform with African political culture since African culture values the collective over the individual.

It is undeniable that classical liberalism is an ideology that took roots in European society. However, unlike Continental European liberalism, classical liberalism is not a Western by-product because it is not an ideology conceptualized strictly for a certain group of people according to their race or religion. Instead, it is an ideology and system conceptualized around the individual.

The essence of classical liberalism is based on the fact that the individual is the unit of measurement for all social institutions and human activities. The individual, regardless of his cultural background, ethnicity, race, and religious values; can only be free if the state exerts a less significant role in his life. This principle is not a Western principle, but a universal principle. The reason why the United Kingdom, the United States, and Australia have a higher degree of freedom and prosperity than most of the countries of Continental Europe, is not because classical liberalism is a Western system that works for them, but because the individuals have more freedom in these countries than in Continental Europe. They have more political and economic freedom.

Classical liberalism has even worked lately in Japan, although Japan is not culturally a Western nation. The reason why Japan is among the most prosperous nations on earth despite not being a Western nation, is simply because, politically, Japan has embraced the rule of law. The rule of law governs the Japanese political system, and economically, the living standard of the Japanese people is significantly higher than most non-Western countries because the Japanese citizens have a high degree of economic freedom.[1] In a nutshell, Japan is today one of the wealthiest

---

[1] 2019 Index of Economic Freedom. *The Heritage Foundation,* (2019) Data.

countries because it has been using classical liberalism as its political and economic model of development. The great question here, is to know; if classical liberalism has worked for the Japanese despite the fact that Japan is neither a Western country, nor that it has a Western culture; then why can classical liberalism not work also in Africa?

The response to this question is the sole task of this book. This book seeks to explain why and how classical liberalism can be implemented in African political culture and how it could work effectively on the continent if the African people are willing to accept classical liberalism, not as a Western by-product, but as a social antidote to guarantee the improvement of their own well-being politically and economically.

This book is divided into three major parts. The first part is entitled *Political Freedom in Africa* and it is constituted of three distinctive chapters. The first chapter of the first part is entitled "Political Systems and African Governments." This chapter gives an overview of the political system that each African government has adopted. The second chapter, entitled "The Rule of Law in African Political Culture," expounds that the political instability engrained in African political culture is due to the absence of the rule of law and the lack of democratization of political institutions. The third chapter of the first part of this book is entitled "Political Rights for the People." This chapter accentuates on the fact that the political rights of the African people are undermined because their government prevents them from exercising their political rights as members living in a civil society. This chapter further explicates that political rights are essential for the good functioning of any civil society as well as they ensure political stability if they are exercised.

The second part of this book is entitled *Economic Freedom in Africa* and it contains three chapters. The first chapter of the second part is entitled "The Problem of African Socialism." This chapter assesses the failure of socialism in Africa and how it has impoverished the continent. The second chapter of the second part of this book is entitled "Private Property and Capital." This chapter seeks to explain the importance of private property and how it is the primary resource to stimulate economic growth and to promulgate a sustainable development. The third chapter of this second part is entitled "The Improvement of the Living Standard in Africa." This chapter illustrates the methods or means that need to be used in order to improve the living standard of many African countries.

A Manifesto

The third part of the book is entitled *"Civil Liberties in Africa"* and it is composed of two chapters. The first chapter of this third part of the book is entitled "Liberty and African Political Culture." The purpose of this chapter is to explain how the concept of civil liberties is still applicable in Africa although African culture is a collectivist culture. The second chapter of this third part, which is also the last chapter of the book, is entitled "Political Authority and African Citizen." This chapter expounds the relationship between the legitimacy of political authority and the freedom of the African citizen in a civil society.

Classical Liberalism in Africa

8

PART I

POLITICAL FREEDOM
IN AFRICA

Classical Liberalism in Africa

CHAPTER 1

POLITICAL SYSTEMS AND AFRICAN GOVERNMENTS

The African continent contains fifty-four countries. The 1960s marked a turning point in African history. It marked the end of European colonization, and the commencement of the independence and post-colonial era.

The majority of African countries during the 1960s, obtained their sovereignty and adopted a political system significantly different from Western liberal democracies. The political system of each African country was an authoritarian and oppressive political system based upon a one-party system. South Africa, which is today the most advanced nation in Africa, has also had a one-party system until the 1990s like the rest of other African countries. Whether it was in Côte d'Ivoire, Ghana, Kenya, Algeria, Guinea, the Democratic Republic of Congo also known as Zaire, Namibia, Ethiopia,

Tanzania, and many more; each of these countries mentioned had a single-party system in which the government which was leading society, was in fact a political party. In order to comprehend the nature of authoritarian government that was generated during the post-colonial era, it is first and foremost essential to fathom the origin of authoritarianism itself.

The theoretical framework of authoritarianism was conceptualized in the *Leviathan* of Thomas Hobbes. In the *Leviathan*, Hobbes explained that, as the state of nature is a place where total anarchy is the master of society, where the lack of law and order permeates the rationale of man, and where the absence of property rights was the main common dominator that determined the nature of the Hobbesian state of nature; it was imperative for individuals to create a society wherein their rights would be protected by the sovereign. In the Hobbesian conception of civil society, the sovereign is the entity that possesses the ultimate power to enforce the laws that it seems adequate to govern society. For Hobbes, the sovereign is the enforcer and the guarantor of the law. The sovereign exists through a covenant established between the people who willingly accept to surrender their rights to a higher authority who will retain political and legal power in exchange for granting security to the citizens.

A Manifesto

The particularity of the sovereign in the Hobbesian conception of civil society is that, the powers of the sovereign are not divided into different branches of government, but they are concentrated into one single branch—whatever that branch may be. In other words, the powers of the sovereign according to Hobbes must neither be divided nor limited but absolute.[2]

The reason why Hobbes believes that the powers of the sovereign must be absolute, is because absolute authority enables the sustentation of political and social stability through law and order. The Hobbesian conception of political authority gives no place to the concept of separations of powers sharing equal powers.

Moreover, it rejects the idea of checks and balances because for Hobbes, checks and balances are a mere impediment for an effective enforcement of civil policy. For Hobbes, only a government that possesses the essential rights of sovereignty can be reliably effective, since where partial sets of these rights are held by different bodies that disagree in their judgments as to what is to be done, paralysis of effective government, or degeneration into a civil

---

[2] "Hobbes's Moral and Political Philosophy: 8. Absolutism" *Stanford Encyclopedia of Philosophy*. Originally published in 2002. Updated in 2018.

war to settle their dispute, may occur.[3] The Hobbesian concept of political power is the philosophical concept from which African leaders have chosen to establish their political system; authoritarian system where the powers of the sovereign are unlimited and unchecked.

It is evidently unsurprising to witness why Africa, throughout the twentieth century, was a politically unstable place. The governments established were either a presidential system, or an absolute monarchy as it was the case in Morocco, Lesotho, and Swaziland. The rest of African countries have had a republican form of government. The republican form of government established in African countries were not truly republicans in the proper sense that we would understand it here in the West. They were only republican in theory because each of these African countries have a written constitution that explicitly underlines the doctrine of separation of powers. However, in practice, the republican form of government was in fact government as an absolute monarchy whereby the sovereign was ruling like a republican monarch. In every African country that has adopted a republican form of government, each of these countries, except for South Africa, have had a strong executive branch while their the

---

[3] Ibid.

legislative and judiciary branches have been significantly weakened.

African presidents consolidated their political power by making the executive branch a tool of absolute power and control. The legal powers of the legislative and the judiciary were simply meaningless, and subverted. For the fact of the matter, political authority was concentrated in the hands of the leader himself, who would govern mercilessly, and had no regards for the principles that the constitution enumerated. For example, Mobutu Sese Seko, the former ruler of Zaire; ruled singlehandedly over his country and his people for thirty-two years with an iron fist. He was the one to appoint the legislators in parliament and the magistrates in the courts. The courts would interpret the laws according to Mobutu's desires,[4] and any attempt to oppose his authority was ruthlessly and perniciously admonished without concession. Mobutu was the perfect illustration of the Leviathan of Hobbes and the Prince of Machiavelli. Mobutu was, by no means, the only African ruler who governed his people autocratically and oppressively. Sekou Touré, Kwame Nkrumah, Julius Nyerere, Jomo Kenyatta, Muhammar Ghaddafi, Houphouët-Boigny, Samuel

---

[4] "Dangerous Dictators: Mobutu Sese Seko" *Searching in History.* Article.

Doe, Charles Taylor, José Eduardo Dos Santos, Jean-Bédel Bokassa, Gnassingbé Eyadema, Idi Amin Dada, and many other leaders; have ruled their respective country autocratically, and to an extent; tyrannically. These leaders have led their people undemocratically, with a monarchic style. African governments, since their post-colonial inception, have been the epitome of utter coercion.

It is undeniable that the concept of African government is authoritarian, sometimes it can be totalitarian. The authoritarianism practiced in the majority of African countries has generated a major political instability in these countries. African head of states succeeded each other not through the democratic process of the peaceful transition of political power, but through coup d'état. For example, in Togo, Gnassingbé Eyadema overthrew Sylvanus Olympio in 1963 through a military coup, which lead to the assassination of Olympio.[5] In Liberia, Samuel Doe overthrew and assassinated William R. Tolbert in the 1980s and Doe himself was overthrown and assassinated by Charles Taylor in 1990.[6] The political instability that has been for so long the cataclysm of African politics, has

---

[5] Editors "Gnassingbé Eyadema" *The Times*, (2005). Article.
[6] Marmon, Brooks, "25 years after his demise, Samuel Doe continues to cast a long shadow across Liberian politics" *African Arguments* (2015). Article. Web.

doomed the continent to a predicamental political recovery because the rule of law was utterly absent from the culture of the transition of political power. The first reason for a society to lag is grounded upon the lack of political stability and the lack of political stability is engrained in the absence of the rule of law. Without political stability, no society can adequately flourish.

CHAPTER 2

THE RULE OF LAW IN AFRICAN POLITICAL CULTURE

The lack of political stability in Africa is indeed ingrained in the absence of the rule of law. The rule of law is the fundamental precept of classical liberalism. It is the precept that determines the ability to enhance economic freedom and civil liberties. Without the respect for the rule of law, economic freedom and civil liberties cannot occur. The precept of the rule of law is in fact a culture. It is a culture that societies have developed over time. It has been widely misbelieved that wealthy nations such as the United States, the United Kingdom, Germany, Australia, Japan, France, Canada, South Africa or Hong Kong; are wealthy simply because they are developed. For the least, this has been the African perception on the matter. The wealth that developed nations have achieved over time, is not a hazardous fact. It was a social behavior converted into becoming a tradition. The reason why wealthy countries are industrialized and developed is not because they are rich in natural resources and that they have developed these resources. They are industrialized because they have developed a culture for the respect and obedience to the rule of law. Their respect and obedience to the rule of law has allowed them to develop access to economic opportunities and it has strengthened their civil liberties. It was not the other way around. Political stability is a necessary condition for economic growth and the expansion of civil liberties to sustainably occur. What has been explained so far is that the rule of law is the fundamental precept that determines the ability to enhance economic freedom and civil liberties. Yet the rule of law itself has not been defined. What is the rule of law and what role it has to play in African political culture?

According to *Encyclopedia Britannica*, the rule of law is the mechanism, the process, institution, practice, or norm that supports the equality of all citizens before the law; secures a nonarbitrary form of government; and more generally prevents the arbitrary use of power.[7] Arbitrariness is typical of various forms of despotism, absolutism, authoritarianism and totalitarianism.[8] In general,

---

[7] Choi, Naomi, "Rule of Law." *Encyclopedia Britannica.* Political Philosophy.
[8] Choi, Ibid.

the rule of law implies that the creation of laws, their enforcement, and the relationships among legal rules are themselves legally regulated, so that no one; including the most highly placed officials; is above the law.[9] The legal constraint on rulers means that the government is subject to existing laws as much as its citizens are.[10] This is the fundamental principle of classical liberalism, and it is the fundamental principle that industrialized nations have followed ever since in order to economically, politically and socially develop themselves.

This fundamental principle that guarantees societal prosperity has never really been implemented in Africa. In fact, it has been dismissed. Our African political leaders, during the post-colonial era, have failed; sometimes purposefully in order to consolidate their own power and pursuing their own interests; to inculcate the precept of the rule of law to their people. Evidently, African political culture is substantively different from Western culture. Nevertheless, the concept of the rule of law is color blinded. It is not a European or a Western cultural feature but a human-nature feature. The non-Western societies that have prioritized the rule of

---

[9] Choi, Ibid.
[10] Choi, Ibid.

law above anything else, have become over time significantly advanced politically, economically, and socially. The question here is to know why Africans failed to embrace the ideal of the rule of law if the rule of law is not in itself an intrinsic European or Western cultural feature, but a social concept bounded to human understanding?

African political culture is a social custom that rotates around the notion of "submission to authority." Indeed, Africans have an embedded belief in authority and tradition. The respect for authority is unequivocally a good social characteristic to have, however, it has one significant flaw. The flaw is that, blind and unconditional respect for authority undermines the rationality of the individual and empowers the authority-holder to not have his actions checked or contested if logic requires so. The problem is that when the authority-holder is never challenged or questioned; this logically and unavoidably leads to a totalitarian society where only the authority-holder becomes the absolute figure to which everyone must submit to, even if the latter makes decisions that do not benefit the common good. The unconditional submission to authority has been the substantial impediment of African political culture.

Since no one dares to contradict or challenge the authority of the authority-holder, then the authority-holder assumes that he has the legitimacy to excessively use his authority and believes that he will not be held accountable for it. This has been the essence of the thoughts of African leaders, and that is why post-colonial Africa has generated countless dictatorships all around the continent.[11] For example, Mobutu has killed half of his fellow countrymen for the mere reason that he wanted to consolidate his power. Mobutu, in a nutshell, eliminated his political opponents physically, and deprived of his or her civil liberties, any Zairian citizen who would dare to challenge his authority or question the action of his government. Mobutu's philosophy about the enforcement of authority was not unique to him. This philosophy was enforced in every post-colonial independent African country. That is why, every African country was governed as a one-party state with repressed political and civil rights.[12] African political leaders did not want to inculcate the idea of the rule of law in their respective country because they well-knew that doing so would jeopardize the legitimacy of

---

[11] Skinner, Elliott P. "African Political Cultures and the Problems of Government" *African Studies Quarterly*, Volume 2, Issue 3 (1998). Article.
[12] Skinner, Ibid.

their authority and the consolidation of their power.

The rule of law is the essence of any sustainable political system and the central characteristic to ensure political stability in any given civil society. Without political stability, there can be neither economic growth nor expansion of civil liberties. The embracement of the rule of law as a cultural feature and key component of African political culture is imperative to ensure the economic and political development of the continent. The most adequate way to properly inculcate the culture of respect and obedience for the rule of law for Africans, is to strengthen the legitimacy of political institutions by applying the principles of separations of powers diligently and rigorously. The effectuation of the principles of separation of powers will, first and foremost, provide an equalization of powers within each branch of government. The equalization of powers of each branch of government will evidently prevent one branch from becoming more powerful than the other two as it has been previously the case in African political history and culture. Let us not forget that in a society governed by the rule of law, the law is the supreme element that governs society; not men. Therefore, it suggests that the equalization of powers between the branches of government is embodied by the legitimization of the law as the decisive factor of governance.

African governments since the post-colonial era have been governed not by the law but by men. African leaders used the authority of the office they hold to subvert the legitimization of the law. That is why most African societies have been politically lagging. Because the law was not the ultimate judge, but the authority-holder was. The authority-holder is a man, and men are fallible beings. It is because men are fallible beings that the law is needed; to confine that fallibility since the law is infallible. In addition to the effectuation of the separation of powers doctrine, the rule of law ensures the peaceful transfer of political power from one incumbent authority-holder to the prospective authority-holder. Ghana and Senegal have been two great examples in West Africa whereby the peaceful transfer of political power has been conducted within the bounds of the law. For example, in 2012, then-incumbent Senegalese President Abdoulaye Wade ran against Macky Sall and lost the presidential elections. Instead of contesting the results because he did not like it, President Wade conceded and peacefully and democratically transferred power to now-incumbent President Macky Sall. In Ghana, a similar scenario had also taken place. During the 2016 election, which opposed then-incumbent

President John Mahama who was running for reelection, and now-incumbent President Nana Akufo-Addo, President Mahama lost and conceded to Nana Akufo-Addo. Here too, the peaceful transfer of political power from one authority-holder to another, has occurred within the scope of the rule of law.

Third, the effectuation of the rule of law incentivizes members of society to willingly become law-abiding citizens. In fact, the rule of law epitomizes the ethical aspects of society. As government is subjected to comply to the existing laws to which the citizen is also subjected to, it encourages the citizen to abide more by the law because he knows that the political authority that governs him is also subjected to these same rules. The effective rule of law requires that citizens comply with the regulatory rules enshrined in the law and enforced by legal authorities.[13] A law-abiding society is one in which people are motivated not by such fears, but rather by a desire to act in socially appropriate and ethical ways.[14] It is then the role of the state to lead by example; by

---

[13] Tyler, Tom R. and Darley John, "Building a Law-Abiding Society: Taking Public Views About Morality and the Legitimacy of Legal Authorities into Account When Formulating Substantive law," *Hofstra Law Review.* (2000). Vol. 28. Issue. 3, Article 5.
[14] Ibid.

subjecting itself to the regulatory laws that it enforces upon the citizenry in order for the citizenry to willingly abide by these same regulatory rules. For example, South Africa, Ghana, and Senegal are three prominent African law-abiding societies where the separation of powers is duly respected and properly enforced; where the peaceful transfer of political power between authority-holders is operated; and where citizens and political officials are subjected to the same regulatory rules. The implementation of the separation of powers doctrine, the peaceful transfer of political power from one authority-holder to another, and the willingness for the citizenry to abide by the existing laws that govern society; are the three key components that determine the political stability of any politically organized society.

The rule of law is not inherently a characteristic solely designed for Western culture. It is an ideal, a social and political principle that is applicable to any politically organized society that is reasonably open-minded to progress and political, economic, and social development. Western nations understood that for them to be free and prosperous, they must assure to themselves that political stability was to be imposed before they could develop their respective economies. African nations that have also followed this recipe, are today freer than countries that are still refusing to embrace the rule of law as a cultural feature of their society.

CHAPTER 3

POLITICAL RIGHTS FOR THE PEOPLE

Political rights are an essential feature of the principles of civil liberties. Civil liberties, overall, established the various liberties that an individual possesses in a civil society such as the right to retain private property, the right to start an economic venture, the right to life, the right to decide for oneself to live his or her life as he or she sees fit…etc. These are some of the elemental rights that an individual possesses in a civil society under the concept of classical liberalism.

Political rights precisely articulate on what an individual is entitled to do politically. It emphasizes upon the participation of the individual into the political action of civil society. The right to vote, the right to freely assemble, the right to sign a petition, the right to create a political party, the right to question and challenge the government's action, the right to protest…etc., are some examples of political rights granted to an individual living in a politically organized society. These political rights are common in free societies whether it is in the United States, the United Kingdom, Japan, Hong Kong, Brazil, South Africa, Canada, or Senegal, or even Ghana. Political rights are preponderant because they enable the citizen to directly participate in the political process of the implementation of civil policy.[15] It gives access to the citizen to oversight the legal procedure operated by the political process.

In Africa, political rights have been drastically scarce although many African governments have made the effort to expand it to their citizens. For example, countries like Kenya, Senegal or South Africa have a higher degree of individual freedom and political rights than the majority of African countries.[16] The reason why political rights have been scarce in Africa, overall, is because, as it was previously explicated in the erstwhile chapter,

---

[15] "Freedom Slipping: Africa's closing political space marked by less freedom and a willingness to trade liberties for security" *Afro Barometer.* (2019). Johannesburg, South Africa. Article. Web.
[16] Campbell, John, "Declining African Confidence in Exercising Political Rights" *Council Foreign Relations.* (2019). Article. Web.

A Manifesto

African political leaders did not like to see their authority and political action being contested.

One way to ensure that their authority would not be challenged was to significantly restrict the political rights of their people. That is why African states, from 1960 to 1990, were all one-party states instead of adopting political pluralism. Political opposition parties were banned. For example, in Côte d'Ivoire, Laurent Gbagbo has been jailed several times, and even sent to exile in the early 1980s for showing a vehement opposition to the power of Houphouët-Boigny and for ceaselessly criticizing the policies of his party; the Democratic Party of Côte d'Ivoire. In 1982, Gbagbo clandestinely created the Ivorian Popular Front in France until President Félix Houphouët-Boigny legalized it in 1990 under the multi-party system. The one-party system that existed in Côte d'Ivoire was not unique to the Ivorian political system. For the fact of the matter, the one-party system was implemented in every single African country from the independence era until the Fall of the Berlin Wall and the collapse of the Soviet Union in the early 1990s.

African political leaders were hostile to granting political rights to their people because it was a way to deprive the citizen of accessing the political realm. Depriving the citizen from participating into the political process was a method to contain him from disrupting the political power of the authority-holder. The constitutions of African governments are based on the principle of positive rights,[17] i.e. rights that are granted to the citizen by the approval of the political authority. Let us remember that the essence of modern African civil society is built upon a Hobbesian social contract in which the sovereign, which in this case is the state, has the ultimate authority to either grant or deprive the citizen of his freedom. Consequently, the nature of African constitutions is inherently coercive. They are meant to expand the power of the state rather than constraining them like the United States has done so, at least in theory. Since African constitutions are inherently Hobbesian, the allowance of political rights in Africa is not a God-given right like it is perceived in the United States or in the Anglo-Saxon world. Political rights in African civil societies, are unfortunately conditional whereby the state detains the only legitimate authority to enforce them or to restrict them. It

---

[17] Positive rights are a concept in political philosophy that argues that the rights that an individual possesses are rights that have been granted to him by the state rather than by God or a divine power above the power of the state. Positive rights suggest that the citizen only has access to them if the state allows him to access them otherwise, these rights are not natural or inalienable to him like it is conceived in the United States or in England.

means that these rights are negotiable, therefore volatile.

Furthermore, the hostility of African political leaders to granting political rights to the citizenry is based upon the need for political authority to control the mind of the masses. If the citizenry had access to political rights, it would have been too rebellious, and it would have fragilized the authority of the leader. African political leaders have failed to develop a culture of constitutional personality[18] within African political culture. The reason of this failure is because political rights are enunciated in the constitutions, and if African political leaders made their people accustom to the rights that their constitution enunciates, they could use that against political authority if the political action being effectuated does not promulgate the interest of the masses. Developed countries, regardless of their cultures, have successfully inculcated to their citizens a constitutional personality in which each member of their society abides by and is protected by.

Some countries in Africa like Ghana, Senegal, South Africa or Kenya; are already known to be

---

[18] Constitutional personality means that a society lives and act by the principles of its constitution promulgates. It substantiates the attachment that a society has the rules established in the constitution.

well-established African democracies because political rights are valued and enhanced. It is utterly preponderant to comprehend that the reason why these African countries known to be democracies in a continent that has been lagging politically, is because these countries have made of the rule of law, the basis of their political system.

When a society makes of the rule of law the foundation of its political system, it signifies that it agrees to grant to its members, access to the political process through the enforcement of political rights. For example, Kenya is considered to be a democracy in Africa because the rule of law became the foundational framework of its political system. Indeed, in Kenya, the rule of law is assured by the impartiality of the judicial branch. The judiciary in Kenya plays a quintessential role because it is the organization that facilitates the access of the citizen to the knowledge of his rights. For a citizen to participate in the political process, he shall be aware and knowledgeable of the constitutional rights that have been granted to him. It is true that many Kenyans remain unaware of their basic rights.[19] This lack of knowledge of their

---

[19] Kameri Mbote, Patricia and Akech, Migai "A. Knowledge of rights-Access to Justice." *Kenya: Justice Sector and the Rule of Law.* (2011). Open Society Initiative for Eastern Africa. P.156. Article.

rights remains a major hindrance to accessing justice, especially among poor, vulnerable, and uneducated people.[20] However, the Kenyan judiciary has made significant efforts to share the knowledge of the constitutional rights of the people with its citizens since the country has adopted political pluralism. Today, political rights in Kenya are stronger than in the majority of African countries. Interestingly, the African countries that have been politically instable, have been so because their lack to establishing the rule of law. And that failure for establishing the rule of law has impeded the access to political rights. The Kenyan people understood that the rule of law is the foundation of political rights. There can be no political rights without the rule of law.

The African continent as a whole, can be a free place where political and economic prosperity can thoroughly germinate. For the economic and political prosperity to sincerely germinate, the African political culture should be opened to embrace the principle of the rule of law as the core value to ensure that the political rights of the African people, wherever they are on the continent, are enforced and ensconced. Our political leaders must be willing to democratize the political institutions of their respective nations if they want

---

[20] Ibid. p. 156.

the sovereignty of their people to be ascertained. Without the democratization of political institutions, citizens cannot exert their political rights and participate in the political process. Classical liberalism is the philosophy that the African political culture must embrace if it wants to ensure that political stability becomes a permanent phenomenon in Africa.

A Manifesto

PART II
ECONOMIC FREEDOM IN AFRICA

CHAPTER 4

THE PROBLEM OF AFRICAN SOCIALISM

It has been widely, vividly, nonetheless, wrongly believed that socialism is the adequate system to improve the living standard of Africa. Worst, it has been misleadingly believed that socialism is compatible with African culture because African culture is fundamentally a collectivist culture. However, one fact remains undisputable, which is that socialism has deliberately failed wherever it was tried, and the African countries that have experimented socialism were not exempted from its failure.

The undeniable fact remains that Africa has the lowest living standard of all continents after Antarctica. The reason why the living standard of the majority of African countries is so low compared to the rest of the world, is because socialism has impoverished the African continent. At the outset of the post-colonial era in the 1960s; many African countries such as Tanzania, Angola, Mali, Ethiopia, Ghana, Mozambique, Egypt,

Senegal, Guinea, Congo and many more; have embraced socialism as their economic and political system. These countries that have embraced socialism became significantly poorer by the 1980s. For example, Tanzania was one of the fast-growing economies in East Africa until Julius Nyerere implemented the Ujamaa, which means socialism and brotherhood in the Swahili language. Before the implementation of the Ujamaa; Tanzania had relatively the same GDP as South Korea.[21] Subsequently to the implementation of Ujamaa, economic growth became unsurprisingly stagnant. The policy of collectivization impoverished the Tanzanian people. Food production fell, and the country's economy suffered.[22] This decline in productivity has made Tanzania one of the poorest countries on the continent. In Ghana, under the rule of Kwame Nkrumah, one of the foremost African political leaders of the post-colonial era; socialism was also effectuated as the economic system of the country. Socialism as a domestic policy in Nkrumah's seven-year development plan, was to be pursued toward "a complete ownership of the economy by the state."[23] A bewildering of

---

[21] World Bank Data of GDP per Capita Growth (Annual %).

[22] Thompsell, Angela, "Socialism in Africa and African Socialism" *ThoughtCo.* (2019). Article. Web.

[23] Ayittey, George. "How Socialism Destroyed Africa" *African Liberty.* (2019). Article. Web.

legislative controls and regulations were imposed on imports, capital transfers, industry, minimum wages, the rights and powers of trade unions, prices, rents and interest rates.[24] Private businesses were taken away and nationalized by the Nkrumah government.[25] The result has also been unsurprising. Resources were mismanaged, inflation rose, and economic stagnation occurred in Ghana. Zimbabwe has also suffered from the myth of African socialism under Mugabe's rule. Mugabe collectivized the means of production in the late 1980s when he became Zimbabwe's strongman. Rampant corruption, huge budget deficits, and mismanagement of resources have dragged the economy, hyperinflation, 60 percent of unemployment rate, and a desperate shortage of hard currency.[26] Figure 1 shows how socialism increased unemployment rate in Zimbabwe from 1999 to 2011. Unemployment rates hits an all-time high, at 95 percent in 2009 before it declines in 2010 and beyond.

---

[24] Ibid.

[25] Ibid.

[26] Meldrum, Andrew, "Mugabe Returns to Socialism" *The Guardian*, (2001). Article. Web.

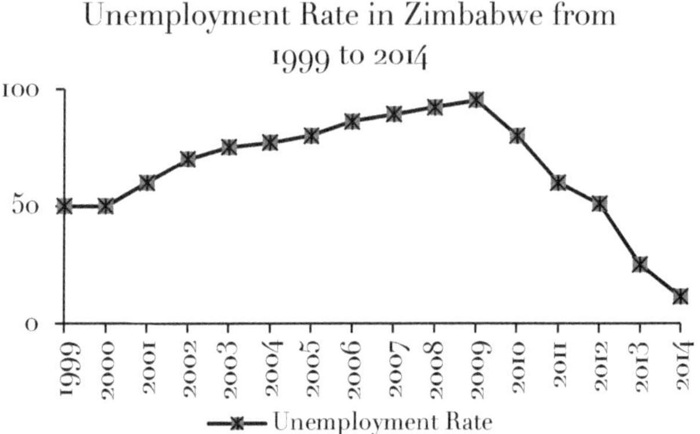

Figure 1. Source: CIA World Factbook. Note: this entry contains the percent of the labor force that is without jobs. Substantial underemployment might be noted.

These examples clearly demonstrate how socialism had utterly stagnated the economies of these countries until a market economy was once again reinstated. The question is why Africans deeply believed in socialism and embraced it in the 1960s?

In Africa, socialism was presented as an anti-colonial and anti-imperialist ideology while capitalism was perceived as the ideology of the oppressor, the colonizer, and the ideology of profit. Africans strongly believe in socialism because they think that socialism is compatible with African culture since African culture is a collectivist culture. African culture values the group over the individual. It values the concept of sharing, solidarity, and altruism. Of course, all these moral virtues are well-intended, but they play no substantial role in the improvement of the living standard of people. What improves the living standard of people is the ability to retain private property, to voluntarily exchange with one another what we own in order to create capital. Some African countries in the post-colonial era resisted the socialist temptation; notably countries like Côte d'Ivoire, Kenya, or South Africa. For example, in the 1960s and 1970s, Côte d'Ivoire was the most economically advanced country in West Africa. While its neighbors were embracing socialism, Côte d'Ivoire opted for a market economy. Despite having an authoritarian political regime, like all African countries did at that time; the Ivorian people were, nonetheless, economically free. From 1960 to 1979, the GDP in Côte d'Ivoire grew at 8.1 percent per year, which means that in real terms capita, it increased from $595 to $1,114[27] as figure 2 illustrates this augmentation.

---

[27] Abbott, Philip, "Agriculture's role in the economy" *Distortions to Agricultural Incentives in Côte d'Ivoire,* (2007) p.9. Department of Agricultural Economics. Purdue University, West Lafayette. Article. Web.

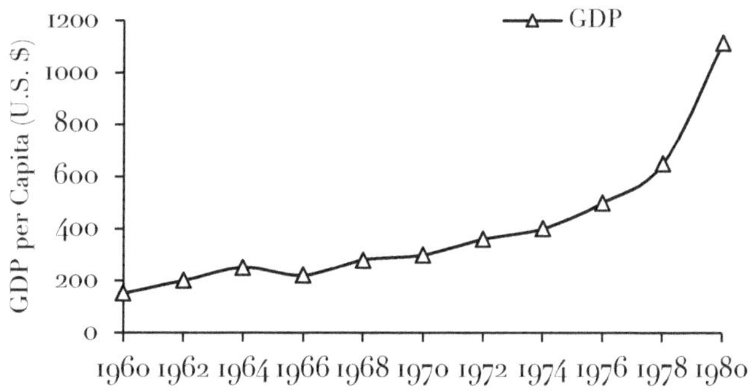

Figure 2. Source: CEI Data

Cote d'Ivoire's economic expansion during that period was called "The Ivorian Miracle" because the country was exporting agricultural goods to its neighboring countries which had a shortage of food production due to their socialistic policies. The Ivorian Miracle made Côte d'Ivoire the most prosperous nation in West Africa between 1960 and 1980.

What Africans have failed to grasp about capitalism and the free market is that, it is not a system intrinsic to Western culture. It is a system intrinsic to human nature regardless of race, ethnicity or the culture of people. Socialism has failed in Africa as it has failed in Eastern Europe, India, China and in South America. Even if Africa is culturally collectivist, it is important to comprehend that a group is only a collectivity of individuals whereby each individual within the group is stimulated by the pursuit of his own interests. The pursuit of one's self-interests is an intrinsic factor of human nature that no central authority can change regardless of the goal of the common good. Despite the collectivist nature of African culture, African culture is not exempted from that natural law of human nature. Coercing human nature to do something that is not in harmony with the nature of human understanding will result in failure. That is why socialism, wherever it is tried, will always fail.

46

CHAPTER 5

PRIVATE PROPERTY AND CAPTIAL

Private property is one of the essential characteristics of economic freedom within the concept of classical liberalism. Strictly speaking, 'property' is a general term for the rules that govern people's access to and control of things like land, natural resources, the means of production, manufactured goods, text, ideas, inventions, and other intellectual products.[28] Property can be tangible such as land or natural resources, or intangible such as ideas, texts, or intellectual products. The term 'private property' means that the ownership of a tangible or intangible resource is not legally bounded to a governmental entity. The right to private property is the fundamental resource of the principle of economic freedom because it represents the element that allows and facilitates the action of economic exchanges between two parties who willingly agree to enter

---

[28] Editors, "Property and Ownership" *Stanford Encyclopedia of Philosophy.* (2004).

into a transaction. Private property is significantly important because it determines access to resources for the development of the means of production. In other words, private property is quintessential to determine the factors of the means of production because without private property, no one can know the value of a resource and how that resource can contribute to the acquisition and accumulation of capital. The truth of the matter is that the retention to private property is a necessary condition to acquire capital because without private property, resources cannot be used as capital to determine production.

Incrementally to the rule of law and the political rights granted to citizens, developed nations are industrialized precisely because they have a considerably higher degree of access to private property than the rest of the world. For example, Hong Kong is considered to be the freest society in 2019 according to the Index of Economic Freedom of the Heritage Foundation. Indeed, Hong Kong has the highest degree of access to property rights with a 93.3 percent rate.[29] Interestingly, Hong Kong is not a Western society and it is economically freer than the United States or the United Kingdom. According to the same data, the most economically

---

[29] "Honk Kong 2019 Index of Economic Freedom" *Heritage Foundation.* (2019). Data.

free country in Africa is Rwanda, with a percentage of access to private property at 72.2. percent.[30] Although Rwanda is economically free, political rights remain restricted. The law in Rwanda recognizes and protects all property rights whether tangible or intangible.[31] Furthermore, property registration was made easier in 2018 for its accessibility.[32] Figure 3 shows a comparison between Rwanda and Kenya on the access to property rights.

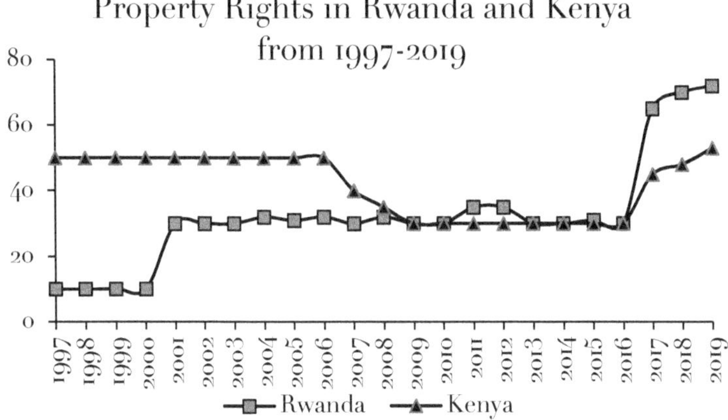

Figure 3. Source: International Property Rights Index. Note: Property rights include physical and intellectual property.

---

[30] "Rwanda 2019 Index of Economic Freedom" *Heritage Foundation* (2019). Data.
[31] Ibid.
[32] Ibid.

Despite the lack of concrete political rights in Rwanda, Rwanda is among Africa's least corrupt countries and is ranked eighth in the world in the Transparency International's 2017 Corruption Perceptions Index.[33] It substantiates that the rule of law is clearly in motion in Rwanda, and it is clearly a matter of time before it becomes as well politically free. As Milton Friedman used to say: *"Economic freedom is a necessary condition for achieving political freedom but not a sufficient condition."* If Rwanda; a country that was once devastated by a horrendous civil war; has been able to recover from it to the point of even becoming one of the freest economies on the African continent, then why cannot other African countries do the same? Figure 4 shows the comparison between Rwanda and Kenya in economic output.

---

[33] Ibid.

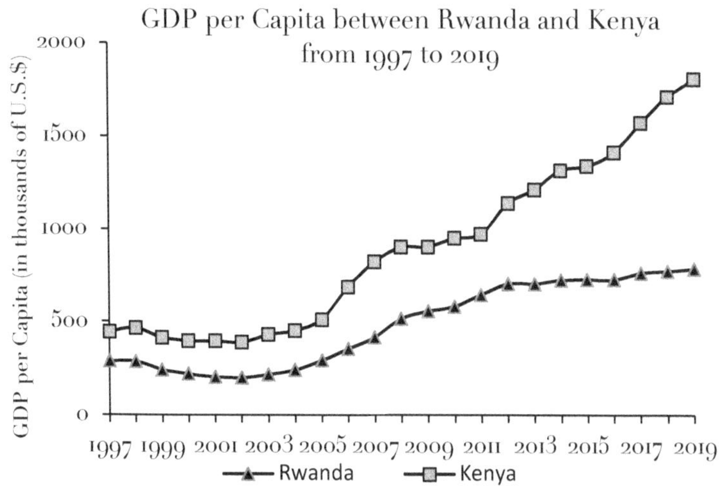

Figure 4. Source: World Bank Data

Even though Rwanda has a higher rate of access to property rights than Kenya overall, Kenya has a higher GDP per capita than Rwanda because no ethnic conflict or genocide has happened during that time while the very same war was happening in Rwanda at the precise time. It is noteworthy to reiterate that the economic recovery of a country following a war is a slow process that takes several months and sometimes years before the economy as whole comes to a full equilibrium again. Figure 3 and 4 clearly substantiate that there is a direct correlation between access to property rights and economic growth.

The economic development of a nation is deep-seated in the accessibility to private property. While Rwanda and Kenya are economically thriving, countries like Liberia, Zimbabwe, the Democratic Republic of Congo, Sudan, Chad, Mozambique or Algeria;[34] are economically impoverished and heartbreakingly repressed because their government has substantially restrained access to private property to their people. It is fundamentally imperative to comprehend that access to private property enables economic growth to occur. For the fact of the matter, private property and economic freedom allow people to coordinate their activities while engaging in trades, which make them both people better off, gives us an indication of the institutional environment that is necessary for prosperity.[35] Private property provides the incentives for individuals to economize on resource use because the user bears the costs of their actions.[36] When private property is combined with market exchange, the price system that results provides the information and incentives for the many anonymous individuals in society to

---

[34] "Country Rankings 2019 Index Economic Freedom" *Heritage Foundation.* (2019). Data.
[35] Powell, Benjamin, "Private Property Rights, Economic Freedom and Well-Being" *Mercatus Center George Mason University.* (2002). P.1. Article. Web.
[36] Ibid. P. 1.

coordinate their activities to channel available resources to the people with the most urgent demand for them.[37] For capital to be created and to be used effectively in order to generate production, individuals in a politically organized society shall be free.

Once again, the concept of private property is not a by-product of Western culture but a by-product of human nature. As it was aforementioned in this essay, the freest society on earth today is not even a Western society but an Asian one. That means that the concept of private property and economic freedom are not a concept strictly applicable to Western societies but to any society that simply wishes to let its members be free to undertake, to create, to stimulate and to innovate economic incentives.

What Africa needs first, is to develop its human capital. Indeed, human capital is the primary resource that enables the utilization of resources. Humans apply their knowledge and skills onto a resource, and the application of knowledge and skills onto a resource is what determines the value of that resource. That being said, African societies need to heavily invest in their human capital in order to expand their access to private property.

---

[37] Ibid. P. 1.

Secondly, it is important that African governments facilitate the people's access to private property as well as its role in economic activities. It is evidently clear that economic and political freedom both require a lesser role of government. Certainly, in economic activities, if the government has the monopoly of major industries, it is generally pernicious for economic growth to occur because the inefficiency of the political process would impede the natural process of economic growth to ensue as more people have had access to private property. Access to private property engenders more economic opportunities and the expansion of economic opportunities develops the expansion of capital. Industrialized nations are industrialized because they have created economic opportunities through the utilization of private property and the expansion of human capital, and the accumulation of capital stocks.

A country like the United States remains the first economic power in the world, not because it has an abundance of natural resources, but because it has designed a system whereby economic opportunities would incentivize people from all around the world to come to the America and to contribute to the economy by sharing and applying their knowledge and skills to the productive powers of labor. The African countries that are today economically advanced, have fathomed that economic opportunities are the recipe to improve the economy of a society and to ameliorate its living standard.

56

CHAPTER 6

THE IMPROVEMENT OF LIVING STANDARD IN AFRICA

The improvement of the living standard of a civil society occurs when the economic system of that society is liberalized; which means that the government does not play a significant role in the regulation of economic activity. Economic liberalism is essential for the development of a civil society for two principal reasons. The first reason is that it attracts human capital through the creation of economic opportunities and the second reason is that economic liberalism expands the access to private property and access to private property authenticates the amelioration of living standard.

In Africa, the living standard of the majority of Africans is significantly low. The sad truth is that the African continent has the lowest living standard among all the continents on the planet. The reason for such deleterious reality is that most African societies have not liberalized enough of their economy. Indeed, when we speak of living standard, it does not limit itself solely to economic activities although economic activities are essential for the improvement of living standard. Social institutions such as education, healthcare, and housing; are also preponderant in the incrementation of living standard. For example, Liberia is one of the poorest countries in Africa for several reasons. Though, the main reason is that the civil war has devastated the economy and Liberian society as a whole. A 2011 study conducted by Human Rights Center of the University of California, Berkeley-School of Law substantiated that only 39 percent of the Liberian people have access to housing, 47 percent of the population has access to water, 43 percent has access to food, 47 percent has access to farmland.[38] However, a striking 79 percent of the general Liberian population has access to work opportunities.[39] It shows that there are incentives to stimulate economic growth although the human capital is lagging because people lack the knowledge to adequately use their skills in order to stimulate economic growth. The high rate of work

---

[38] Vinck Patrick, Pham Phuong, Pham, Kreutzer Tino, "Talking Place: A Population-Based Survey on Attitudes About Security Dispute Resolution, and Post-Conflict Reconstruction." *Human Rights Center University of California, Berkeley-School of Law.* (2011). Data.
[39] Ibid.

opportunities, and the low rates of access to basic needs show that in Liberia, government and central-planning economics are not the primary responsible for the low living standards of the Liberian people, but the war, the destruction of economic output, and the reduction of human capital; have had pernicious long-term consequences upon the economic development of Liberia. Figure 5 illustrates the economic growth in Liberia from 2001 to 2018. The data clearly substantiates that economic growth in Liberia has been slow through the years and has been in decline in the mid-2010s.

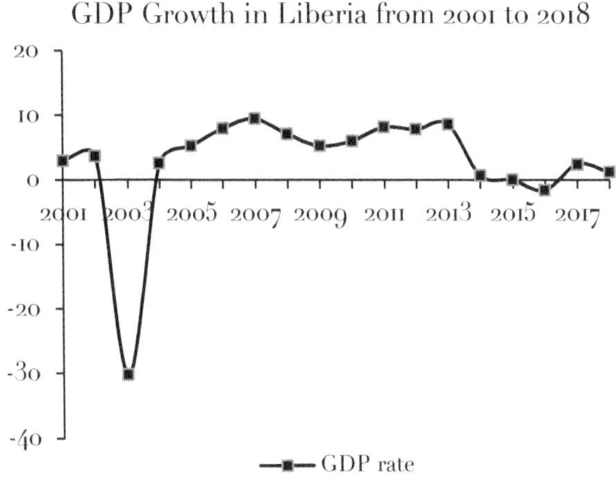

Figure 5. Source: World Bank Data

Liberia is evidently not the only poor country in Africa where its living standard is borderline catastrophic. Chad is also among the poorest nations of the continent, and the main reason of this extended poverty is rooted in the substantial lack of human capital. According to a study conducted by the World Bank, Chad occupies the last place on the Human Capital Index.[40] Indeed, A child born in Chad will be 29 percent less productive in adulthood than a child who received a quality education and benefited from appropriate health services.[41] Moreover, although Chad had made progress on poverty reduction, with a decline in the national rate from 55 percent to 47 percent between 2003 and 2011, but the number of poor people was projected to increase from 4.7 million to 6.3 million between 2011 and 2019.[42]

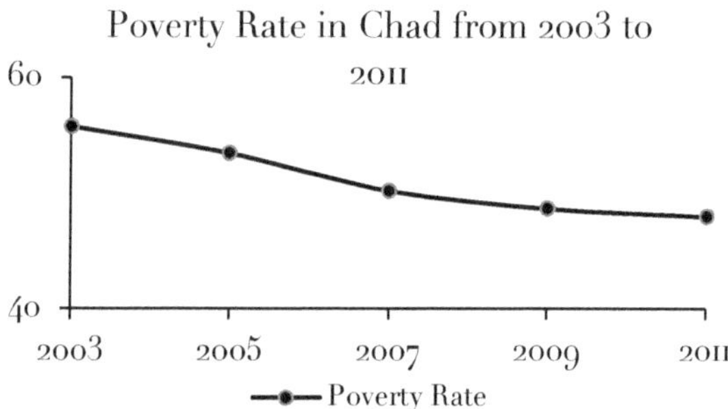

Figure 6. Source: Poverty Gap Index/Our World in Data

---

[40] "The World Bank In Chad" *The World Bank.* (2019) Data.
[41] Ibid.
[42] Ibid.

The poverty striking in Chad is based upon the lack of human capital, capitalism, and economic incentives. Figure 7 illustrates a comparison between the average rate of economic freedom in Chad and that of the rest of the world. The data shows that Chad is ranked among the most repressed countries in terms of economic freedom, which is averaging 50 percent compared to the rest of the world whose rate is averaging 60 percent. According to the Index of Economic Freedom, a country is considered for the least free if it scores above 60 percent on average.[43] Undeniably, geography has a role to play upon the backwardness of the Chadian economy. Nonetheless, as human capital in Chad remains drastically low because it is in significant shortage, productivity is, therefore, less and the economy as a whole, struggles to expand.

---

[43] 2019 Index of Economic Freedom, *The Heritage Foundation*

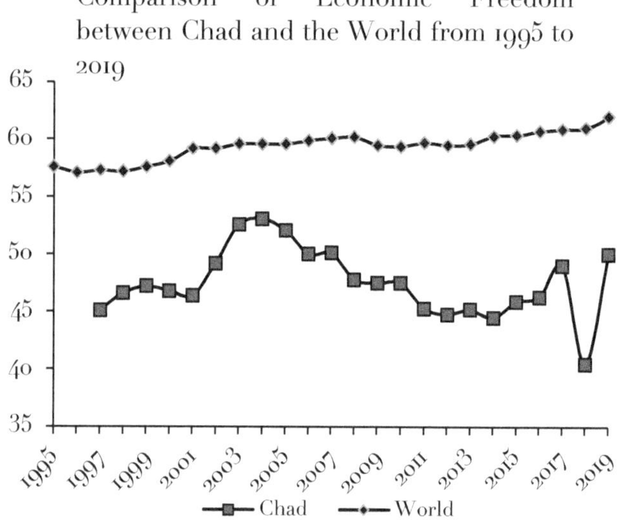

Figure 7. Source: Index of Economic Freedom, The Heritage Foundation

Capitalism and the market economy are the economic system that have enriched every modern society. The productive capacity to create wealth is what has made some societies more prosperous, including some African countries, than other societies that are politically and economically lagging. The improvement of the living standard of a society, regardless of its cultural values and heritage, is based upon the development of human capital. The population of the whole African continent today, is over a billion people.[44] It signifies that the African continent does have an

---

[44] African Population, Data.

extensive human capital, a human capital relatively equal to that of China, and India, which both have over a billion inhabitants; and a human capital three times higher than that of the United States, which has a population of 325 million inhabitants, and higher the whole European continent which has an aggregate population of 741 millions of inhabitants.[45] Furthermore, according to the Brookings Institute annual report on population growth, 60 percent of Africa's 1.25 billion people are under age 25, which is the youngest population in the world.[46] The fact that Africa has a population of over a billion inhabitants with its two-third being constituted of individuals of age 25 and below, indicates that the human capital is not only abundant but it is also young, dynamic and innovative-driven. However, despite this young and booming population, the living standard in Africa remains low. Why?

Most African leaders have recognized nowadays that for economic development to take place, they must loosen the government role in the economy of their respective countries. That being said, they finally understood that they must open their economy to local entrepreneurs, foreign

---

[45] European population, Data.
[46] Dews, Fred, "Charts of the Week: Africa Changing Demographics" *Brookings Institute,* (2019). Data.

multinationals, and foreign investors. They have finally recognized that only a market economy with very few regulations, could be the solution to improve the living standard of the African population. Among the 1.2 billion of Africans living within the continent, 600 million of them do not have access to electricity.[47] To provide that access, many African governments have agreed to let entrepreneurship flourishing in their countries. For example, in February 2014, Senegalese-American songwriter, Akon; launched the Akon Lightning Africa Initiative also known as Solektra.[48] Evidently, the purpose of the project was to facilitate access to electricity for African populations living in rural areas. Following the launching of this entrepreneurial project, Solektra has been active with 200 thousands small projects, providing electricity in fourteen African countries including Mali, Niger, Senegal, Guinea, Burkina Faso, Sierra Leone, Benin, Guinea Equatorial, Republic of Congo, Namibia, Madagascar; Kenya and Nigeria.[49] Thanks to Solektra, some African populations were able to have access to electricity, therefore, have an improvement of their living

---

[47] Adegboye, Emmanuel, "Entrepreneurship—A Pathway to Sustainable Development" *Medium,* (2018), Article. Web.
[48] Thurston, Charles W. "Rapper Akon Lights Up Africa With Solar," *PV Magazine,* (2017). Article. Web.
[49] Ibid.

standard in their local communities. By using private means to supply basic public goods to the general public, Akon was able to develop the human capital that contributed to the distribution of electricity throughout these fourteen countries. Many people were then employed subsequently to the launching of Solektra, which helped them being lifted out of poverty and having a better living standard. Another example can be enunciated to demonstrate that capitalism is what the African continent needs for a sustainable development as well as an improvement of the living standard.

In 2012, The Welsch company founded a model that could provide clean water to the East African region. Starting relatively small, with projects, their goal was to increase the availability of clean drinking water; the Welsch company decided to focus not just on the problems of poor infrastructures and water supply, but also on supporting local entrepreneurs and job creation.[50] This initiative would evidently enable local entrepreneurs to develop the human capital in that region. For the fact of the matter, by 2020; the Welsch company with local entrepreneurs, aim to provide a million people with access to safe

---

[50] Coates, Jessie, "Innovative Approaches in East Africa are Overcoming Structural Challenges to Provide Clean Water— And Build a better Future" *EY.* (2018). Article. Web.

drinking water and help create 1,000 locally-owned businesses and 8,000 jobs.[51]

Capitalism, entrepreneurship and a market economy are what determine the improvement of the living condition of a given society regardless of where this society is located, and regardless of its cultural values. Economic freedom cannot be enhanced if members of society are not free to voluntarily exchange the resources that they privately owned. But for members of society to freely exchange the resources they privately owned; the state must let them do so. The state shall not intervene at a greater extent in order for the living conditions of the most vulnerable members of society, to improve. What improves the living condition of men and a society as a whole; is the creation of employment, economic opportunity, the facilitation of having access to private property, freedom to enterprise, undertake, and innovate. This is how the living standard of the most vulnerable members of society improves.

---

[51] Ibid.

PART III

CIVIL LIBERTIES IN AFRICA

CHAPTER 7

LIBERTY AND AFRICAN POLITICAL CULTURE

Liberty, in its most fundamental sense, is the state of being free within society from oppressive restrictions imposed by authority upon one's way of life, behavior, or political views. In short, liberty is the absence of coercion. As it was expounded in the introduction of this book, classical liberalism is a political ideology founded in Europe whose core doctrine is based upon liberty. The principle of liberty establishes the relationship between the individual and the society in which he lives in, that is to say, the relationship between the individual and the institutions and laws that govern civil society.

The fundamental precept of classical liberalism is that the individual is the basic social unit within society. This indicates that the institutions and laws that govern civil society according to classical liberalism, are actually effectuated according to the fulfillment of the individual. Since classical liberalism advocates for the freedom of the individual as the source of its ideal, it then means that the individual, according to the classical liberal principle, is in itself an end rather than a means to end. For classical liberalism, individual fulfillment is the finality of men's quest for freedom, and this freedom can be achieved if man is free from coercion whether it is by government or other forms of authority that impose restrictions on behavior and civil conduct.

The basis of classical liberalism is fundamentally and undeniably different from the basis of African political culture. While classical liberalism sees the individual as the basic social unit, African political culture sees the individual as means to an end rather than an end in itself. African political culture perceives the individual as a means to an end because African tradition argues that the preservation of the common good, in other words, the collective; is the highest moral purpose of the African man, and that the role of the individual is to contribute to the fulfillment of the common good. For Africans, the welfare of the group is more important than the welfare of the individual because the individual only has value if and only if the group is fulfilled. Therefore, in African political culture, the group is the basic social unit. And when we say the group, we actually mean the community.

The community as a whole has more essence than each individual does. The concept of African political culture is founded on the ideals of equality, fair share, altruism, and the attachment of man toward his community. Africans are culturally accustomed to value the well-being of one another. By valuing the well-being of one another, it means to monetarily provide for the person who needs assistance. In African culture, it is a moral obligation that those who have the means to help and empower the disenfranchised, must do so because it signifies that they are contributing to the fulfillment of the common good; therefore, they are supporting its betterment. This moral obligation culturally inculcated to African people correlates with the reasons why Africans have an infallible obedience for authority. A very basic example is the fact that a typical African person embedded in African tradition, will never contest or challenge the authority of the chief of his community or ethnic group whether the decisions of the chief may be controversial or harmful to the welfare of the community as a whole. Africa is inhabited by various ethnic nationalities with their different language modes of dressing, eating, dancing, and even greeting habits that are absolutely different than Western customs.[52]

In African culture, as it was previously enunciated, the haves have a moral obligation to assist the have-nots. It is a default customary prerequisite of the cultural setting of Africa while in Europe and the Western world, the individual has the moral obligation to assist himself primarily before assisting anyone else. In other words, in European and Western culture, the individual owes nothing to his community while in African culture, the individual owes everything to his community. It is palpably limpid that Western cultural values and African cultural values are considerably antagonistic to one another. If they are antagonistic to one another, how can we then reconcile the concept of liberty with the fundamental values of African political culture?

The truth of the matter is that, a community is, first and foremost, made up of individuals. Each individual being a member of the community has, nevertheless, his own aspirations, desires and goals that he seeks to achieve or fulfill. Human nature leans naturally towards liberty one way or another, whether consciously or unconsciously, because

---

[52] Idang, Gabriel, E. "African Culture and Values" *UNISA*, Phronimon, Volume 16, Number 2 (2015) pp.97-111. Department of Philosophy, University of Uyo. Article.

human being himself is a living being endowed with reason who utilizes his ability to reason in order to determine the trajectory of his development and fulfillment. The conundrum with the basis of African political culture, which is to value the needs of the community over that of the individual, is that it impedes the individual to adequately help his community. Because, in order to help someone, one must acquire the means first, before helping the one in need. But how the one who is presumably supposed to help his fellow man and his community, can do so if the community that he is supposed to serve prevents him from acquiring the means to supply the help needed by imposing upon him a set of restrictions and demands that undermine his ability to help? Western nations are considered to be selfish; in particular the United States. To an extent, this assertion is valid but not in its entirety.

In fact, the American political culture, contrary to the African political culture, is highly individualistic because the "I" prevails over the "we." The essence of American political culture could be conveyed as "I shall enjoy the fruit of my labor because what I make belongs to me." It underscores a certain selfishness, but it is not a selfishness based on mere greed. It is a rational selfishness, a selfishness based on rational choices made by the individual that lead to concrete and beneficial outcomes. The presumed "selfishness" of American political culture is embedded in the concept of the right to property, which was elucidated by Locke in *Second Treatise of Government.* The validity of American individualism and "selfishness" is grounded upon the fact that labor is the basis of private property. "He who works the land rightly deserves to appropriate himself the portion of land that he has cultivated." This is the Lockean theory which justifies the concept of liberty according to classical liberalism as well as individualism in Western culture in general and that of the United States in particular. In contradistinction, the African political culture is highly inherently collectivist because the "we" prevails over the "I."

The essence of African political culture could be conveyed as the following: *"What you have achieved does not solely rest upon your own effort. Your achievement is thanks to the contribution of the community that has helped lifting you in order for you to be where you are today."* This concept, somewhat, aligns with the general catchphrase pertained in the United States that everyone colloquially vowed "You didn't build that!" The essence of African political culture forces the individual to recognize that there is a higher power above him, and that power is the togetherness of his community, and the togetherness of his community is what has helped him achieved what he has achieved. Consequently, he is morally obliged to give back to those who have contributed to his success. This approach is evidently as equally valid as the individualism of the West.

Nonetheless, the problem with the collectivist approach that determines African political culture is that it has generated a custom of cultural dependency. For example, in a conventional African family with many children and low economic means; the parents will choose among their many children, the child that is slightly above average, which means, the child who showcases a promising successful future. The parents will then put all of their hopes in that child by sending him to Europe or to America for a better life. The parents are relatively old enough, and the siblings of the child being sent abroad, are young and able-bodied. By sending that child to a foreign land, the parents and the child's siblings, all expect the child to send some money home as soon as he obtains a job and his first paycheck. Moreover, they expect the child to send money recurrently to his family regardless of the kind of job he does, regardless of how much he makes, and regardless of the conditions under which he performs the job. If the child failed to send money, his family may reprimand him. Such attitude clearly reflects two obvious facts. The first fact is that the child being sent to Europe or America, is not mentally free. He does not work to fulfill himself but works to fulfill the needs and desires of his parents and siblings. In other words, the child's life and labor is being exploited by his own people. The second fact is that the child's parents and siblings all became dependent on the income of the child working abroad. They all look forward to his income to be redistributed to each of them regardless of the amount of income tax and bills he has to pay. In sum, the collectivist culture in which the child working abroad grew up into, has enslaved him to morally and monetarily owe individuals, who like him, are able to create income for themselves, and therefore help their parents as well.

It is tremendously preponderant for the African people to comprehend that liberalism is not merely a by-product of Western civilization. For the fact of the matter, it is a by-product of human nature. It is a by-product of human nature because it advocates for the individual to be free regardless of his cultural values, ethnic background, or religious values. Having access to economic and political rights should not be perceived as a European or Western cultural feature but as a logical and human-nature feature because man without liberty cannot adequately develop himself no matter what his skin color, religion and ethnic background is or could be.

A Manifesto

It is obvious that man needs certain rules of social conduct in order to maintain civility and respect for human existence. However, it is also important and wise that the authority, which is upholding civil order, does not abuse its power. The problem with political authority is that, it constrains the ability of the individual to be free in a civil society as it enforces more rules and regulations upon him. It is principally one of the reasons why African societies are governed autocratically rather than democratically and liberally.

The concept of liberty should be promoted in African political culture, not to decimate the roots of African culture, but to complete and to add more value to African culture. Without a certain extent of liberty, whether it is in the political or economic realm, the living standard in Africa as a whole cannot significantly improve like it has improved in countries like Singapore, South Korea, Japan, Hong Kong, Rwanda, South Africa, Kenya, Malaysia; are examples of non-Western countries that have today a higher degree of freedom in their respective societies. Liberty is something that can be inculcated into African political culture and compatible with African culture as a whole to an extent.

78

CHAPTER 8

POLITICAL AUTHORITY AND THE AFRICAN CITIZEN

In order to understand the concept of political authority and the role that it plays in African civil society; one must, first and foremost, fathom the historical period of Africa that preceded the independence.

The African continent was mostly dominated by the two main colonial powers which are France and the United Kingdom. Of course, Portugal has colonized Angola, Mozambique, Cape Verde, Guinea Bissau, Equatorial Guinea, and São Tome and Principe.[53] The Arabs, who mainly originated from the Middle East, colonized North Africa from Morocco to Egypt, but also, Mauritania, Sudan, and Somalia. The Dutch, at some point, did colonize Southern Africa, especially some parts of South Africa and former Rhodesia now known as

---

[53] Richard, Katherine Schulz, "The Portuguese Empire" *ThoughtCo.* (2019). Article. Web.

Zimbabwe. Notwithstanding, France, and the United Kingdom were two European powers that have left a significant impact upon African political culture up to today, and these two countries did colonize the majority of African countries.

France and the United Kingdom did impact the legal, and political systems of the African continent. This impact, indeed, has essentially determined the political cultures of French-speaking African countries and English-speaking African countries. The noteworthy and blatant difference between the two is that the majority of English-speaking African countries are more politically and economically advanced than French-speaking African countries. It does, by no means, indicates that every single English-speaking African country is more developed than any single French-speaking country. For example, Côte d'Ivoire, which is a French-speaking African country, is politically and economically more advanced than Liberia which is an English-speaking African country. The point here is to simply understand why, overall, English-speaking African countries have a steadfast and better political and economic development than French-speaking African countries.

During the colonial period, France and the United Kingdom have implemented two different legal and political systems upon their colonies; and these systems became the political heritage of African countries, a heritage that has undermined the original political tradition that existed in Africa before the colonial period. The British colonial system was based upon an indirect rule or indirect administration over its colonies. The indirect rule is a system of governance in which the colonial power exerts political authority over its colonies by delegating some of its powers to the local indigenous rulers of indigenous communities who are supervised behind the scenes by the advisors of the colonial power.[54] The central feature about the indirect rule is that it sought to preserve tradition and allowing some flexibility for local authorities to make up their own rules so long as these rules remained conformed with the ideology of the colonial power.[55] For example, indirect rule was first used by the British in Africa in Buganda, Uganda; then developed it in Northern Nigeria, later extending it to other colonies on the African continent.[56] The Uganda Agreement of 1900 clarified that Bugandans were to be governed by

---

[54] "What was Indirect Rule?" *General History.*

[55] Lawrence, Adria, Associate Professor at Yale University, "Colonial Approaches to Governance in the Periphery: Direct and Indirect Rule in French Algeria." *Colonial Encounters and Divergent Development Trajectories in the Mediterranean,* Harvard University, (2016). Article.

[56] "What was Indirect Rule?" *General History.*

hereditary rulers.[57] These made laws in accordance with the British Governor.

The essential characteristic of the concept of indirect rule is based upon the decentralization of political power. English political tradition has always been that political power should not be centralized in the hands of the ruler, but that this power should be delegated to local authorities, who can exert a greater influence on the local populations since these authorities are having a direct contact with the local populations. Therefore, local authorities have a better understanding of the needs of what the local populations want and can implement policies according to their realities. This political tradition being carried on by English-speaking African countries reflects that the political system in these countries is conventionally less centralized.

On the other hand, France applied a direct rule over its colonies. The direct rule is a system of governance in which the colonial power exerts political control over its colonies by appointing rulers who are directly from the colonial power and these appointed-rulers are sent in the colonies to enforce the policy of the colonial power upon the local indigenous populations. For example, the

---

[57] Ibid.

governor-general in Dakar, who was the appointed-ruler from France in Dakar, Senegal; was to report to, and take his orders from the Minister of Colonies and the government in Paris.[58] To an extent, the direct rule is actually similar to the Soviet command-style economy, in which the Soviet government directly decided how economic policy should be enforced upon the Soviet people. Advocates for direct rule envisioned a colonial project that would modernize and transform colonial territories.[59] Proponents of the direct rule argued that autochthone populations were incapable to modernize themselves because they were too ingrained into their traditions. Their reluctance and unreceptivity to modernize themselves could not occur unless a central authority exercises substantive power over them in order to force them to accept the new concept being presented to them. The French did not utilize traditional power holders in their administration of

---

[58] Wooten, Stephen, "French in West Africa: Early Contact to Independence" *University of Pennsylvania-African Studies Center.* Article.

[59] Adria, Lawrence, Associate Professor at Yale University, "Colonial Approaches to Governance in the Periphery: Direct and Indirect rule in French Algeria" *Colonial Encounters and Divergent Development Trajectories in the Mediterranean,"* Harvard University, (2016). Article.

the colony to any greater extent contrary to the British.[60]

The direct rule installed by the French, was a centralized federalist administration in which the state exerts a significant control over the populations it has subjugated while the indirect rule favors some flexibility of political power over local populations. Undeniably, the direct rule was the political legacy bequeathed to the French-speaking African countries. Today, the political system of most French-speaking African countries is highly centralized with major restrictions on what an individual can do or not do.

The colonial heritage that has shaped African political culture, did unequivocally determine the political system of African countries. African countries that were subjugated to a direct rule, have today less freedom for their citizens. For the fact of the matter, the centralization of a political system of a society, to a greater extent, affects perniciously the economic system of that society. Societies whose political authority is considerably expanded, have the rights of the citizens basically marginalized. Political authority controls access to economic

---

[60] Wooten, Stephen, "French in West Africa: Early Contact to Independence" *University of Pennsylvania-African Studies Center.* Article.

opportunities as well as it controls the factors of social advancement.

Economic opportunities and social advancement are the two principal factors that should not be determined by a central authority for the mere reason that political authority is unable to adequately comprehend the needs of each single individual within the society it governs; consequently, political power is incapable to adequately supply those needs. A country like Cameroon, for example, is governed like the French direct rule. Political power controls many aspects of the life of the Cameroonian citizens. That is why Cameroon is not politically nor economically advanced. The Cameroonian citizens are not politically nor economically free. According to the 2019 Economic Index of the Heritage Foundation, Cameroon is ranked among the societies that are mostly unfree because the rule of law is deficient, access to private property is scarce, therefore the people living in Cameroon are not free vis-à-vis the political authority in Cameroon. Somalia is another example whereby political authority is a total failure and where there is no prospect for political and economic freedom in whatsoever possible way. Somalia is a failed state wherein its political and legal institutions are utterly dysfunctional. Anarchy is the system that currently reigns in Somalia. The citizens are clearly not free because there is no political authority to secure the rights of the people in Somalia.

The African citizen can be a free man if he finally comprehends the scope of the role of political authority in his life. Most Africans do not understand the limitations of political authority over their lives because they have not been educated to think that way.

A Manifesto

CONCLUSION

Here comes the end of our analysis. After reading the three parts of this book, the reader has, by then, fathomed that classical liberalism is not an ideology only manufactured for "white people" but for any society that aims to become self-sufficient, i.e. for everyone regardless of skin color or cultural basis. Some may say that Arab countries such as Saudi Arabia or Qatar, are economically prosperous without having political freedom. That is, indeed, a valid argument. However, Saudi Arabia and Qatar, are only economically free. They are not politically nor socially free. Women have limited rights, and slavery is still a legal institution in these countries, especially in Saudi Arabia. The economic prosperity of Arab countries is not primarily based on their people but upon the commodities they use as natural resources such as oil. Venezuela today is paying the price for having relied on its natural resources rather than its people. Venezuela, which was once one of the most advanced economies in South America is today on the brink of collapse.

Classical Liberalism in Africa

Many Africans countries have done significant progress in sixty years of political existence, to be where they are today. Rwanda, Ghana, Côte d'Ivoire, Kenya, Morocco, Nigeria, South Africa, and Botswana are prime examples of African states that are today prosperous whether it is economically, politically, or socially because they have implemented at least two of the elements of classical liberalism into their political and cultural systems.

As it was aforementioned, classical liberalism is not a political ideology only manufactured for Western culture. It is a concept design for human nature. It is clearly undeniable that human prosperity is fundamentally embedded in individualism to some extent. It does not mean that an individual can only become successful just by himself. Human beings are, after all, social animals. However, for a society to prosper collectively, individuals must primarily focus on their personal endeavor in order to create the necessary conditions for society to benefit from it. And classical liberalism offers these conditions so that the human condition itself could thrive in a free society.

The concept of the rule of law is something that must be taught in schools and included in curriculums as civic course. The lack of the rule of law is what has lagged Africa until today. It is important that Africans learn how to respect legal and political institutions. It is important that African head of states learn how to alternate political power for the enhancement of democratic rules to prevail.

In short, it is important that African governments become limited in order for the African people to thoroughly and sustainably prosper. Without the rule of law, Africa will continue to lag as a society and African states will fail to create economic opportunities for their people.

REFERENCES

1. 2019 Index of Economic Freedom. *The Heritage Foundation*, (2019). Data.

2. "Hobbes's Moral and Political Philosophy: 8. Absolutism" *Stanford Encyclopedia of Philosophy*. Originally published in 2002. Updated in 2018.

3. Stanford Encyclopedia, Ibid.

4. "Dangerous Dictators: Mobutu Sese Seko" *Searching in History*. Article.

5. Choi, Naomi, "Rule of Law." *Encyclopedia Britannica*. Political Philosophy.

6. Naomi, Ibid.

7. Naomi, Ibid.

8. Naomi, Ibid.

9. Skinner, Elliott P. "African Political Cultures and the Problems of Government" *African Studies Quarterly*, Volume 2, Issue 3 (1998). Article.

10. Skinner, Ibid.

11. Tyler, Tom R. and Darley John, "Building a Law-Abiding Society: Taking Public Views About Morality and the Legitimacy of Legal Authorities into Account When Formulating Substantive law," *Hofstra Law Review*. (2000). Vol. 28. Issue. 3, Article 5.

12. Tyler & Darley, Ibid.

13. "Freedom Slipping: Africa's closing political space marked by less freedom and a willingness to trade liberties for security" *Afro Barometer*. (2019). Johannesburg, South Africa. Article. Web.

14. Campbell, John, "Declining African Confidence in Exercising Political Rights" *Council Foreign Relations*. (2019). Article. Web.

15. Positive rights are a concept in political philosophy that argues that the rights that an individual possesses are rights that have been granted to him by the state rather than by God or a divine power above the power of the state. Positive rights suggest that the citizen only has access to them if the state allows him to access otherwise, these rights are not natural or

inalienable to him like it is conceived in the United States or in England.

16. Constitutional personality means that a society lives and act by the principles of its constitution promulgates. It substantiates the attachment that a society has the rules established in the constitution.

17. Kameri Mbote, Patricia and Akech, Migai "A. Knowledge of rights-Access to Justice." *Kenya: Justice Sector and the Rule of Law.* (2011). Open Society Initiative for Eastern Africa. P.156. Article.

18. Mbote, Ibid. p. 156.

19. World Bank Data of GDP per Capita Growth (Annual %).

20. Thompsell, Angela, "Socialism in Africa and African Socialism" *ThoughtCo.* (2019). Article. Web.

21. Ayittey, George. "How Socialism Destroyed Africa" *African Liberty.* (2019). Article. Web.

22. Ayittey, Ibid.

23. Ayittey, Ibid.

24. Meldrum, Andrew, "Mugabe Returns to Socialism" *The Guardian,* (2001). Article. Web.

25. Abbott, Philip, "Agriculture's role in the economy" *Distortions to Agricultural Incentives in Côte d'Ivoire,* (2007) p.9. Department of Agricultural Economics. Purdue University, West Lafayette. Article. Web.

26. Editors, "Property and Ownership" *Stanford Encyclopedia of Philosophy.* (2004).

27. "Honk Kong 2019 Index of Economic Freedom" *Heritage Foundation.* (2019). Data.

28. "Rwanda 2019 Index of Economic Freedom" *Heritage Foundation* (2019). Data.

29. Rwanda, Ibid.

30. Rwanda, Ibid.

31. Rwanda, Ibid.
32. "Country Rankings 2019 Index Economic Freedom" *Heritage Foundation.* (2019). Data.

33. Powell, Benjamin, "Private Property Rights, Economic Freedom and Well-Being" *Mercatus Center George Mason University.* (2002). P.1. Article. Web.

34. Ibid. P. 1.

35. Ibid. P. 1.

36. Vinck Patrick, Pham Phuong, Pham, Kreutzer Tino, "Talking Place: A Population-Based Survey on Attitudes About Security Dispute Resolution, and Post-Conflict Reconstruction." *Human Rights Center University of California, Berkeley-School of Law.* (2011). Data.

37. Ibid.

38. "The World Bank In Chad" *The World Bank.* (2019) Data.

39. Ibid.

40. Ibid.

41. 2019 Index of Economic Freedom, *The Heritage Foundation,* (2019). Data

42. African Population, Data.

43. European population, Data.

44. Dews, Fred, "Charts of the Week: Africa Changing Demographics" *Brookings Institute,* (2019). Data.

45. Adegboye, Emmanuel, "Entrepreneurship—A Pathway to Sustainable Development" *Medium,* (2018), Article. Web.

46. Thurston, Charles W. "Rapper Akon Lights Up Africa With Solar," *PV Magazine,* (2017). Article. Web.

47. Thurston, Ibid.

48. Coates, Jessie, "Innovative Approaches in East Africa are Overcoming Structural Challenges to Provide Clean Water—And Build a better Future" *EY.* (2018). Article. Web.

49. Coates, Ibid.

50. Idang, Gabriel, E. "African Culture and Values" *UNISA*, Phronimon, Volume 16, Number 2 (2015) pp.97-111. Department of Philosophy, University of Uyo. Article.

51. Richard, Katherine Schulz, "The Portuguese Empire" *ThoughtCo.* (2019). Article. Web.

52. "What was Indirect Rule?" *General History.*

53. Lawrence, Adria, Associate Professor at Yale University, "Colonial Approaches to Governance in the Periphery: Direct and Indirect Rule in French Algeria." *Colonial Encounters and Divergent Development Trajectories in the Mediterranean,* Harvard University, (2016). Article.

54. "What was Indirect Rule?" *General History.*

55. General History, Ibid.

56. Wooten, Stephen, "French in West Africa: Early Contact to Independence" *University of Pennsylvania-African Studies Center.* Article.

57. Adria, Lawrence, Associate Professor at Yale University, "Colonial Approaches to Governance in the Periphery: Direct and Indirect rule in French Algeria" *Colonial Encounters and Divergent Development Trajectories in the Mediterranean,* " Harvard University, (2016). Article.

58. Wooten, Stephen, "French in West Africa: Early Contact to Independence" *University of Pennsylvania-African Studies Center.* Article.